dear girl

a poetry collection
for survivors

Karen Thursby

dear girl

Karen Thursby

Copyright 2021 Karen Thursby

All rights reserved. No part of this book may be reproduced or distributed in any printed or electronic form without prior written permission of Karen Thursby, except in the case of brief excerpts included in a critical review.

Cover Design Copyright 2021

For Dax and Skye, my reasons why.

Contents

dear girl	9
unfurling	11
back dives	13
the rabbit and i	17
i can't go home – for 7	21
dear sisters	23
giraffe comes	27
born with one name	31
black curtain	33
a place	37
what you fear	39
invitation	41
dare me	43
poet	47
dear sally	49
breathing in	53
elephant wrinkles	55
my spiral	57
the bird rises	59
transformation	63
recreated	67
shoulder strength	69
Love	73
mothered	75

dear girl

let me give you
  a message dear girl
let me tell you
  the Truth
yes, the Truth
  with a capital T

oh yes, I know the difference,
  dear girl
what they told you
  as they held you
    down –
  programmed you –
were Lies, dear girl
oh yes, dear girl, Lies
  with a capital L

here is my message
  for you
you have the power of
  all the angels
    all the lions
      all the bears
on your side

you have the power of
   Love with a capital L
on your side

oh dear girl
   you are greatly loved
   you are beyond precious
   you will do great things

oh dear girl
   feel my hand
     reaching for yours

unfurling

i am springing forth
  from the chaos
of atoms smashing
unfurling exploding
  coming forth

new to you
  but not new to all
i am a puzzle
  and an answer
all together

not all who
  come from the
wall are
   evil

you say implantation
  and i counter
  with creation
  black magic
   meets
unfurling ferns

fierce, magical things
 can come from the
 dark of the night
  dark of the soil-soul
  dark of the uterus

ask me
 i will tell you

back dives

it was scary
  learning to dive

hands above my
  head
toes to the edge

dani showing saying
  just keep bending
    backwards

trusting that
  my feet would
    follow
trusting that
  i wouldn't
    land flat
bruise my back

it was scary
  learning to dive
    inward too

at first i saw
  a boulder that
needed to
be smashed
so i attacked
  it with a
big shovel

i wanted that
  boulder destroyed
smashed into pieces

my work will
soon be over
  i thought

diving with a shovel
  is not easy

one morning i woke
  standing on the
    diving board
looking at my
  rock

the sun hit
  the diamond

on the inside
   just right

now i jump
   off the side
with tiny hand pick

i chip little pieces
my little finger
   can reach
through the rock
   touch the diamond

it is hot
   radiant
it is life

the rabbit and i

it was from
  the uptown bank
the local
  savings & trust
rewards of a school field
    trip
the year before
  a plastic dog

you know – the early
  lessons
save your money
  and everything will be
    fine

this year
  the take home bank
    came in the form
of a rabbit

grayish brown
  rough hair
dark black plastic
    eyes

it stood on
   my dresser
  peripherally
the night time
   guard

i got lost
  in that eye
a black bubble
   surrounded me
scary safe echoing

that rabbit
  watched over me
watched as you
  came in my room

into that eye
  i'd float
time stopped
  the rabbit & i
    we'd watch

i lost
   my voice
had no mouth
     choked silent

if that
  rabbit could
     talk
you'd
  be in
     prison

i can't go home – for 7

i can't skate
  anymore
my legs are
  tired
my belly is
  empty

mama says
  don't get your
    dress
      dirty

daddy says
  i am a
    dirty girl
pushes me down
while i skate
or walk or live

i can't get up
  i am too
    tired
who tied
  my skates

together?

  where is that
     angel
     with flowers
  to scatter on
     me
  where is the elephant
     wrinkles on
        his knees

  i can't go home

dear sisters

this is what
i want you
  to know
    to remember

you are as important
  as a tree
  as a leaf
  as the sky

this is what
  i want you
    to know
      to remember

you are
  just a small part
of an amazing
  planet
no more important
  than a tree
    than a leaf
      than the sky

do you hear
  that sound?
do you hear
  those drums?
do you know
  they drum
    to protect you?

gather round
  dear sisters
find your roots
just like these
  trees
pick up your
  drum
    your hand
      your heart

circle round
  dear sisters

we have a
  dear one
who needs to feel
  the pulse
of the drum
  in her heart

who needs to feel
   the circle of womyn
the circle of safety
   the circle of protection

this dear one
   is our sister

giraffe comes

i am ready to
  know you
dear Sally

oh yes
  i know
that you cannot
  have
    joy
when all you
  feel is
    terror

has Mary come
  to save
    you
  to be the
    mother
  that didn't
    protect
you
  was she
    left out of
      the ritual

all womyn
   didn't count
not even the
   holy ones
      sacred ones
after all, misogyny
in the 70's is
   much like
      misogyny
      today

made nameless
   faceless
made not to
   remember

in a family
   of six littles
only three were
   holy and sacred

us three girls
   used, abused, and
anything but
   holy

giraffe comes
   to protect you
from all that is
    holy
and unholy

giraffe comes
   to protect you
from mothers who
    don't mother

giraffe comes
   to protect you
  from what was
    and what is

giraffe comes
  giraffe comes
    giraffe comes

born with one name

i was born
  with one name
a name given
  by five siblings

but in the
  night
i was divided
  by evil forces
and evil faces
  and evil deeds

and so i became
  many
hidden deep inside
protectors and
  littles
hidden memories
  hidden parts
afterall, how else
  can you learn
    second grade math?

i owe my life
   to each of you
out of impossible
   darkness
beautiful beings

funny and sad and furious
   flying and running and
     living on the vent
      on the edge
     where the ceiling
      meets the wall

i will say your names
allow me the honor
   please

yellow
   seven
     sally and her tiny friend
teenage boy
   old man and
     they

thank you
   thank you
     thank you

black curtain

the sun is
  setting
the air is
  thick still

walking up
  these stone steps
feels like
  walking through
    knee deep snow

i don't come
  here
as often as
  i used to

my shoulder easily
  pushes
open the
  unlocked door

the smells are
  familiar penetrating
like my father's breath

i wander through
  unused rooms
    tracing my
  way to the
    small
dark back room

one window
  allows
the last of
the sun's rays
to illuminate
the black curtain
  hiding the alcove

pulling the curtain
  i see
the black rotten
  eggs
the shells have been eaten
    away

for years
  i've come
opened the window
  thrown these

eggs

only a few
   remain
i gag when
  i hold them
they crumble
   like feta
  through my fingers

i cup my hands
  to keep its
shape
  place it
back behind
  the
curtain

the wall
  holds me
gates
   open

a place

you are so strong
  she said
attempts to boost
    up
acknowledgement of what
  never should have
    been

maybe some
  i'm glad it was
    you
and not
    me

I have a lot
  of protectors
for the weak and
  strong insiders

i wonder if they
need their own
resting place

a haven at which to
    arrive
a place of solace
a place of refueling
a place to get
    ready
for more plunges and
    dives

a place without a
    leader
a place with flickering
    light
never running out of
    oil
lasting beyond 8 nights
beyond and beyond

what you fear

you see me as
   simple
you running
fear of complexity
  all the same

all the comparisons
  to butterflies
emerging to who
   you are
not giving up
  in the cocoon
    stage

assigning wisdom
  to insects
is laughable

what you want
  for me is
a box with boundaries
  an emergence from
    cocoon
only to live

   one month
      flittering about

what you fear
  is the fire
  the destruction
  the deep roots
no, deeper than that
  core roots
    that bring fire
anarchy disruption

don't tell me
  i'm a
     butterfly

my mouth
  will open
and singe
   your
      eyebrows
your box
  your patriarchy

what you should
    fear
  is me

invitation

i am inviting you
  to the
    pause
  between your
    inhale
  and exhale

to the space
  just outside of
    pain

i am inviting you
  to the
    peace
that comes with
    release

can you hear my
    call?
it comes in the
    stillness
of a lotus flower
  atop a
    ladder

it comes in the
 distant call
  of the
   coyote's cry

i am inviting you
 to take a single
  step

i am inviting you
 to open your
  eyes
 and see all the
  beauty

i am inviting you
 to close your
  eyes
 and feel all the
  beauty

do you accept
 my invitation?

dare me

you have tried
succeeded long
  in burying me
labels
    harsh
  prognosis bleak
kill that spark
"how dare you try to
rise up"

black glass box
  buried deep
    trapped
  air gone
    breath shallow

box shatters
  cutting
    slashing
"how dare you try to
rise up"

waiting for death
believing the words

   you will not rise up
     you will not rise up
       you will not rise up

waiting for the little
  of movement
    to stop
"you will not rise up"
   waiting for stillness

breath of life
  i will not die
will not fade
  will not slink away
to make life
  easier for you

breath of life
  spark from below
how dare you think
  i will die
beneath these
    ashes

how dare you think
  i will not rise

i am a phoenix
  i am rising
    i am the
      phoenix

poet

you are a poet
standing in strength
listening with curiosity

you may turn the
  world on its head
scream your obscenities
  in my ear
    in my direction
      in my body
but you won't rattle me

hands defiant on
  my hips
feathers unruffled

go ahead and
  bare your teeth

look at me
  unwavering
    unflappable

turn me upside down
  and i will right
    myself
  find my hips
  find my source
    find my center

i am a poet

dear sally

let me say
  your truth
let me honor you
with the space
  and time
    and intention
to hear your
  truth
dear sally

i hear you
  you cannot have
    joy
when all you
  feel is
    fear

you cannot have
  joy or peace or
  maybe even a felt
    sense of love
when your very
  existence is fear
    careful watching

    careful movements
    careful words

because if you slip
  out of fear
your worst image may
  become your worst
    reality

and so we
  invite giraffe
  to be our
totem, our safety, our
    guide

she looks out
  tall neck
  able to sense
    danger and safety
and alerts us all

a swift kick by
  long lean leg
will maim the
  evil faces

what i know
   dear sally
is you deserve that
   slide
that jungle gym
   to climb on

what i know
   dear sally
is you deserve
    to be four

what you deserve
   dear sally
is safety so that
  you can feel
    pure joy

breathing in

Breathing in the safety of an elephant's eye
Breathing out the anger of a dragon's fire breath

Breathing in the cool breeze of an elephant's flopping ear
Breathing out the ride on a dragon's back

Breathing in I am safe
Breathing out I am protected

Breathing in I notice
Breathing out I ground

Breathing in earth moving grounded steps
Breathing out thighs clenching a dragon's back

Breathing in I am breathing in
Breathing out I am breathing out

In
  Out

elephant wrinkles

what was sacred
  when i was
    7
  was forced

this, they said,
  is a sacrament
this, they said,
  is holy
and so into the
  box i went
    with the old man priest
      who knew nothing
    of the wholly unholy
    things that happened
      to me from
      his kind
        and from those
      other "fatherly" kind

what sins does a
    7
year old have
to confess?

and so i lied
   i fibbed and thought
of my bike that
awaited after my
     penance

i thought about
   sacred animals
i floated to
   the ceiling and saw
things from where
the wall meets
   the ceiling

i climbed into
   the wrinkles of
     an elephant
felt the breeze
  of the flap of
    his big elephant
       ear

tucked in
by the eyelashes
   of his sacred eye

my spiral

watch me
  rise up
from your
  circle
watch me
  dance
    away
from your
  evil
from your circle
  of torture
your circle
  of death

i am more
  than a phoenix
i am embodied
  in this
    body
i am reaching
  and stretching
and dancing
  away from
    your evil

these circles
  are becoming
  my energy
    my spiral
      of connectivity
  authenticity
    positivity

that damaged
  self
is floating
  away
the one you told
  to die
the one you offered
  to buy a gun
for so that
  the reminder
of your evil ways
  would die
    shrink
      disappear

watch me
  watch me
    rise up

the bird rises

i want to
  know
    you
my little guy
hidden behind
  heavy wooden
    church doors
painted red
  a warning for
    those that
      enter

a big scarlet
    door
a warning for
  what happens
    inside

i'm inviting you
    out
i'm inviting you
    outside

   your eyes
      dart back
  and forth
     back and
       forth

what is safe?
   what can be said?

i've dressed so
   you can find me
i'll raise my voice
   so you can
      hear me

i need you
   to believe
     me

outside the bird
     rises
outside reminders
     to look up

a wing creating
     draft
a wing creating

        space
a wing lifting
     me up
     and out
     and
        away

transformation

come here, sister
it's hard, isn't it?
  diving down
  into the river
    lake
      ocean

do you know
  it may,
  just may,
be worth it
    sister?

magical and
  transformative
things may,
  just may,
    happen

do you know I
  live here
and there
  and well,
    everywhere

I see that ocean
　knocking you
　　right on your
　　　ass

salt water pushing
　into your
　　nose
making you feel
　like you can't
　　won't
　　　breathe

gather yourself, sister

I'm right here
　at the bottom
with a gift for
　you

pick yourself up, sister
　follow the dolphins
　swim down and
　　play
　and come up for
　　air

come touch me, sister
　I live Here

my gift for you
　is transformation

recreated

my dear one
  do you know
you were created
  by my Love

deep from my
  flesh
deep from my
  heart
deep from
  inside
this earth
  this river
    this vessel

where have you
  shrunk to
who is searching
  for whom

i am Present
   ready
my flesh
   can and will
receive you

put your hands
   on mine
     in mine
sink dear one
   into this protection
into this vessel

you can be
   recreated

shoulder strength

35 years using
  all my weight
  all my shoulder
    strength

pushing against
this closet
    door
a junk closet
filled to
    bursting
never meant to be
    opened
or even
    used

if opened
it would be
  a pandora's
    box

if opened
  it would flood
    me

    this house
    this space

if opened
  it couldn't be
    closed

and so i
  worked
80 hours a week
one foot on
  an airplane
one shoulder
  against the
    door
truly believing my
  worth
came from
  productivity

and then
  and then

the door cracked
  from the pressure
of a stampede of
    elephants

and the truth is
  i did drown
  and it did
    flood
and i couldn't
    breathe
    or kick
      or swim

until i could

until wet hair
  and soggy clothed
    me
stood in front
  of that door
took what i
    needed
and left that
    house

Love

Love,
  how will i
    know you?

  how will i
  feel and see and
    be with you?

if i contort myself
  into this pose
    am i closer to you?

if i eat vegan, and cut out
  sugar, and grow a
  garden, will i
    find you then?

what if i read the Bible,
  the Quran, the great
  works, will i see
    you then?

Love,
   how will i
     know you?

if i say the rosary, write
  gratitude lists, and
   kneel all the way
    up these steps,
     then?

if i quit my job and
  walk a path of
  solitude, will i find
   you there?

or perhaps in a commune, a
coffee shop, a temple…

Love, she answers me.
She calls <u>me</u> Love. Can you imagine?

She says, "My dear Love,
  you only have to be."

mothered

i am inviting
    you
to open these
    metal
heavy, leaden
    doors

you will need
  to rise from
    your knees
  rise from your
  thoughts and
    prayers
  to action

i've already been
    failed
by a mother
  who refused to
    mother
refused to
    protect

failed by
   the misogyny
of a church

a church that
   turns womyn
      to stone
   worshipping
      non-action

i am waiting
   for you
   to find me
      to push through
         these doors
with a candle
   to light
      the darkness
with a candle
   to start
      a fire
to warm me
     us

lean into me
    please
i need to be
    found
i need to be
    warmed
i need to be
    mothered

Printed in Great Britain
by Amazon